BIBLE STORIES
FOR
LITTLE CHILDREN

D1203594

BIBLE STORIES FOR LITTLE CHILDREN

VOLUME FOUR, REVISED EDITION
From Job to Nehemiah

---

by Betty R. Hollender

illustrated by Martin Lemelman

UAHC PRESS
New York, New York

Library of Congress Cataloging-in-Publication Data
(Revised for vol. 4)
Hollender, Betty R.
  Bible stories for little children.

      Vol. 4 illustrated by Martin Lemelman.
      An illustrated retelling of the stories found in the Old Testament.

   1. Bible stories, English—O.T. [1. Bible stories—O.T.] I. Bearson, Lee,
ill. II. Lemelman, Martin, ill. III. Title.
BS551.2.H6   1986   221.9′505   85-24708
ISBN 0-8074-0309-1 (pbk. :v. 1)

© 1960, 1989 by the UAHC Press
Manufactured in the United States of America
10 9 8 7 6 5 4 3 2 1

Publication of this book was made possible
by a generous grant from the
AUDRE AND BERNARD RAPOPORT
Library Fund

To my grandchildren—
enthusiastic listeners
B.R.H.

To my brother, Bernard
M.L.

INTRODUCTION

Stories from the Bible are a rich source of Jewish literacy and identity. No wonder, then, that Jews of all ages tell and retell stories of the matriarchs, patriarchs, kings, and prophets.

Children love stories. And what better gift can we give to our sons and daughters than the treasure of Scripture, made accessible to them at precisely the moment they begin to read. In bringing biblical characters to life, in presenting them with all their strengths and all their shortcomings, in emphasizing the values that their lives embodied, we say to our children: You, too, can be a Jewish leader. You, too, can make a difference.

For some three decades, Betty Hollender's *Bible Stories for Little Children* has been read and enjoyed by hundreds of thousands of young people. Now recast in a more contemporary style, Ms. Hollender's stories will enable the study of the Bible for yet another generation.

We are proud to bring this special volume to you, and we hope that it will be widely used in both classrooms and homes throughout North America.

Rabbi Daniel B. Syme

THANK YOU

I wish to thank all the people who made this book possible. Their enthusiasm as well as their contributions have made it a special volume.

Some of these people are: Rabbi Daniel B. Syme, Rabbi Howard I. Bogot, Stuart L. Benick, Aron Hirt-Manheimer, Annette Abramson, and Martin Lemelman, the artist, for his wonderful illustrations.

Thanks also go to my husband, Herbert, who has been an inspiration for all my creative efforts.

Betty R. Hollender

CONTENTS

BIBLE STORIES
FOR
LITTLE CHILDREN

GOING HOME

"Hear ye! Hear ye!"
shouted the king's messengers.
"Hear the words of Cyrus.
Hear the words of the king of Persia:
'God has been good to me.
God has given me the countries of the earth.
God has commanded me…
God has commanded me to build a Temple
in Jerusalem.
All Jews may return to Jerusalem.
They may go back to their own land.
They may build God a Temple.
They may live in their own land once again.'

"'Zerubbabel will be the governor.
I will give him wood to build the Temple.
I will give him gold and silver
to decorate the Temple.
And I will give him the holy cups,
the holy cups from Solomon's Temple.
Nebuchadnezzar took them fifty years ago.
I will give them back.
You will use them in the new Temple.
They will go home with you.'"

"The Land of Israel was the land of our grandparents,"
said some of the Jews.
"But we are happy here.
We have pleasant homes.
We have a lovely synagogue.
We can worship God in Babylon, too."

"Good news," said the others.
"We are going back to the Land of Israel.
Our parents farmed that land.
Our grandparents farmed that land.
We will go back and farm the land, too.

"Nebuchadnezzar conquered our land.
He burned Jerusalem.
He took many Jews with him to Babylon.
Cyrus will give us our land again.
He will let us go back to the land of our grandparents.
And we will go back to our land.
We will go back home with Zerubbabel."
And they did.

THE SECOND TEMPLE

Many people watched the Jews build the Temple.
"Wonderful," said some.
"How quickly they work."
"Terrible," said the others.
"Why should the Jews build a Temple?
If they have a Temple, they will be strong.
They will be our enemies.
They may conquer us.
We must not let them finish the Temple."

"But what can we do to stop them?"
"We will shoot arrows at the workers," said someone.
They shot arrows at the workers.
Many workers were killed.
Many were hurt.
But the Jews kept right on building their Temple.
"If we steal their wood," said someone, "they will not
be able to build their Temple at all."

They came at night, and they stole the wood.
The Jews could not do anything.
They were sad.
They did not know what to do.
"Zerubbabel," they said,
"we do not want to build the Temple.
Our enemies shoot arrows at us.
They kill our friends with bows and arrows.
They steal our wood. We have none left.
We cannot build the Temple."
"Zerubbabel," they said.
"What shall we do now?"

"I will tell you what to do," said Zerubbabel.
"We can still build the Temple.
I will get more wood, and I will put some soldiers
near the Temple.
They will watch our enemies.
They will fight our enemies.
You will not have to be afraid anymore."

"Solomon did not need soldiers,"
said a voice in the crowd.
"He did not use soldiers to build God's Temple."

"Solomon did not have enemies," shouted
Zerubbabel.
"We want to build the Temple,
but they will not let us.
We will fight them.
We will kill them.
Then we will be able to finish our work."
"Oh, no, Zerubbabel," said the voice.
"You do not need soldiers to guard the Temple.
God will take care of you.
God will watch you
while you work and while you sleep.
Hear the word of God, Zerubbabel.
Remember it well.
Not by might, not by power,
but by God's spirit
shall God's house be built in Jerusalem."

Zerubbabel bowed his head.
"I will remember the word," said Zerubbabel.
"And my people will remember it, too.
Put your faith in God, my people.
God will help us build the Temple.
We will not need soldiers.
We will not need arrows.
God will take care of us.
God will help us build the Temple."
And God did.
Sometimes enemies came.
Sometimes they shot arrows at the Jews.
But the people did not stop building.
They did not stop hoping.
And they built God's Temple in Jerusalem once more.

THE WALL BUILDER

Nehemiah was cupbearer to the king of Persia.
He poured his wine.
He made sure that the wine was clean and pure.
"My wine cup, where is my wine cup?"
asked the king one day.
"Here, Your Majesty.
Here is your wine cup," said Nehemiah.
"Thank you," said King Cyrus.
He put the cup to his lips.
"But where is the wine?" he shouted.
"Nehemiah, what is the trouble today?
First you do not bring my wine cup at all.
Then you bring the wine cup,
but you do not pour wine into it.
You are my best servant.
You are a wonderful cupbearer.
You never forget my wine cup.
You never bring me an empty one.
What is the matter?"

"Nothing, Your Majesty.
Nothing is the matter."
"Tell me, Nehemiah," said the king.
"What is troubling you?
Every day you smile.
You make me smile, too.
But today your face is sad.
Let me help you."

"My brother Hanani has come from Jerusalem,"
said Nehemiah.

"You have not seen him for many years,"
said King Cyrus.
"Is he sick?"
"No," said Nehemiah.
"Hanani feels fine,
but Hanani's heart is sick.
And my heart is sick, too.

"I have no wife.
I have no children.
And I never will.
My people are my family.
My people's troubles are my troubles.
My brothers in Jerusalem are sad.
They see the walls of their city broken down.
They see the gates of their city burned to the ground.
They work on the walls by day.
They build them stone by stone.
By night, their enemies take the stones away.
The people have no more hope.
'We have worked for nothing,' they say.
'We will never be safe in our city.
We will never have peace in Jerusalem.'"

"How can I help?" asked the king.
"Let me go back to Jerusalem," said Nehemiah.
"Let me be the governor there.
Let me rebuild it.
Give me wood to make beams
for the walls of Jerusalem.
Give me wood to make new gates for the city."

"All this I give you," said the king, "and more....

I will also give you soldiers and horsemen
to protect Jerusalem.
I will make you governor of the land.
Only remember.
Do not stay forever.
Come back to me in twelve years.
Remember, I need you, too."
"Thank you," said Nehemiah.
He kissed the king's robe.
"Thank you very much."

A STRONG WALL IS GOOD

Nehemiah went to Jerusalem.
He was governor of Jerusalem for twelve years.
"My people are like my children,"
thought Nehemiah.
"I must help them make this city strong.
I must teach them to be brave
and to trust in God."
Nehemiah helped his people
build a wall around Jerusalem.
"Nehemiah," said the people,
"how can we thank you?
You have saved us from our enemies.
They cannot hurt us now.
Our wall is very strong.
They cannot break it down."

"My people," said Nehemiah,
"a strong wall is good.
It will keep your enemies away.
But trust in *Adonai* is better.
God can always guard the city.
Sometimes a wall cannot.
Do you remember our ancestors?
They lived in this land.
They trusted *Adonai*,
and *Adonai* took care of them.
In Babylon, we read the Torah every week.
It tells us about our ancestors.
Abraham believed in God.
God sent him a son.
Moses believed in God.

God led the Hebrews out of Egypt.
David listened to God's word.
God made this country strong.

"Ezra is your priest.
He was a boy in Babylon.
He has studied the Torah.
He brought a Torah with him.

He will read it to you.
He will teach you about our ancestors:
Abraham, Isaac, Jacob,
Sarah, Rebecca, Rachel, and Leah.
He will tell you stories about Moses,
about Gideon, and about Deborah.
He will tell you about King David and King Solomon
who built a beautiful Temple to God.
He will teach you the laws of God.
You will listen to Ezra,
and you will be strong.
For *Adonai* will be with you."
"Read to us now," cried the people.
"Not today," said Nehemiah.
"But come back tomorrow.
Come here tomorrow,
and Ezra will read you the Torah."

WE HAVE MADE MISTAKES

The next day, the people met again.
"Read to us, Ezra," they said.
"Read us the Torah so we can do what is right."
Ezra read the Torah.
The people listened.
"We did not know God's Law," said the people.
The sun rose higher.
The day grew hotter.
Still the people listened.
"We have made mistakes," said the people.
The sun was overhead.
The day was very hot.
But the people listened to every word.
Finally Ezra finished reading.
"We have sinned against God every day,"
said the people.
and they began to cry.

"Do not cry," said Ezra.
"We will read the Torah again.
It will tell you what to do.
Do not be sad.
Go to your homes.
Eat and drink.
But remember the poor.
Send them something to eat.
Everyone must be happy on this holy day.
It is the day we learned about our Torah."
The people listened.
The people heard.
The people began to smile.

"We have a wall," they said.
"And we have a Torah.
Now we can live in peace.
Now we can live like brothers and sisters.
This is a holy day.
This is a happy day,
the day we learned about our Torah."

RUTH

Elimelech and Naomi lived in Bethlehem.
They had two sons.
They were a happy family.
But one year there was a famine.
The wheat dried up.
The olives did not grow.
"Give us some food, Mother," said the two boys.
"We have no food, my sons," said Naomi.
"No one in Bethlehem has food."
"There is food in Moab," said Elimelech.
"But I do not want to live in a strange land.
I do not want my sons to learn
to worship strange gods.
I want them to grow up here in Bethlehem.
I want them to learn God's ways.
It is better to eat in Moab
than have hungry children in Bethlehem,"
said Naomi.

"You are right, my dear," said Elimelech.
"We shall surely starve here.
We will go to Moab.
We will leave tomorrow.
We will worship our God in Moab, too.
We will try to bring up our boys as good Jews."

Elimelech, Naomi, and the two boys
lived in Moab many years.
The boys grew up.
They married lovely girls, Ruth and Orpah.
They were all very happy.

But sickness came to Moab.
Many people became sick.
Many people died.
Elimelech and his sons died.
But Naomi, Ruth, and Orpah lived.
They did not get sick at all.

Naomi was lonesome.
"I miss my husband," said Naomi to Ruth.
"I miss my sons," she said to Orpah.
"I even miss my family in Bethlehem," said Naomi.
"You girls are very kind.
You take good care of me.
But still I am lonesome.
I am going back to Bethlehem."
"We will go with you," said Orpah.
"Yes, Mother, we will go with you," said Ruth.
"No," said Naomi.
"I will go alone.
Moab is your land.
The Moabites are your people.
Your gods are here, too.
This is the land where you belong.
I will go back to Bethlehem alone."

The next morning, Naomi got up early.
Ruth and Orpah got up early, too.
"Let us walk with you to the Land of Israel,"
they said.
"Thank you," said Naomi.
"Let us walk together for the last time."

They all set out for the Land of Israel.
They walked a long, long way.

They walked till the sun was high in the sky.
They came to the end of the Land of Moab.
"Good-by, Orpah," said Naomi.
"I will go with you, Mother," said Orpah.
"I will miss you if I stay in Moab."
"No, child," said Naomi.
"You must stay here.
Your people are here.
Your father's house is here,
and your gods are here, too."
"I will go home," said Orpah,
"but I will miss you very much.
Good-by, Mother."
Orpah turned around and went back
to her father's house.

"Good-by, Ruth," said Naomi.
"I will go with you, Mother," said Ruth.
"No, child," said Naomi.
"You must stay here.
"Your home is here,
and your gods are here, too."
"My home was here," said Ruth.
"My people were here,
and my gods were here, too.
But not anymore.
I want to go with you.
Your people shall be my people,
and your God will be my God."
Ruth kissed Naomi.
And Naomi kissed Ruth.

They went along together
until they got to Bethlehem.

They found Naomi's old neighbors in Bethlehem.
They found a small house to live in.
"We can live here," said Ruth.
"But how will we eat?"
"We Jews have a custom," said Naomi.
"At harvest time we do not take in all our grain.
We leave the corners of our fields
for the poor and the stranger.
If any grain falls, we do not pick it up;
it is also for the poor and the stranger."
"Good," said Ruth.
"I will go in the morning.
I will find a field
where the grain smells sweet.
I will bring the grain home.
And you will make barley cakes
for us to eat."

In the morning, Ruth got up early.
She found a field
where the grain smelled sweet.
"I will gather some grain here," thought Ruth.
She began to work.
The sun got hot.
Ruth was hot and thirsty.
She stood up.
She wiped her forehead with her scarf.

"You must be very hot and tired," said a voice.
Ruth looked up.
A handsome man was looking at her.
"You are a good worker," said the man.
"Why have I not seen you before?"

"My name is Ruth.
I just came to Bethlehem.
I live here with Naomi."
"I have heard about you," said Boaz.
"I have heard that you are a lovely girl.
I have heard that you take good care
of Naomi.
You deserve more grain.
Take what you want.
Stay with my serving girls.
When you are hungry,
come and eat with them.
You will be safe here."
"Thank you," said Ruth.
"You are very kind."

The sun went down. Ruth went home.
"You had a good day," said Naomi.
"You are carrying a lot of barley.
It will make fine flour.
I can make many cakes from it."
"I was lucky," said Ruth.
"I looked for a field
where the grain smelled sweet.
I started to pick up some barley.
A man came up to me.
'Stay with my girls,' he said.
'Gather your barley with them
and eat when you are hungry.'"
"What was the man's name?" asked Naomi.
"Boaz," said Ruth.
"Boaz?" said Naomi.
"You were lucky indeed.

Boaz is our cousin.
He will take good care of you, I am sure."

Ruth saw Boaz often.
"How strong and handsome he is,"
thought Ruth.
Boaz saw Ruth, too.
"How beautiful and gentle she is,"
thought Boaz.
"She will make a good wife.
She will give me strong sons
to honor the Living God," thought Boaz.

And so it happened.
Boaz and Ruth were married.
They had a strong and righteous son.
His name was Obed.
Obed had a strong and righteous son.
His name was Jesse.
And Jesse, too,
had a strong and righteous son.
His name was David.
He became ruler of all Isreal.
The Star of David was named for him.

Hear, my child, the discipline of your father,
And do not forsake the instruction of your mother.
Proverbs 1:8

GO TO NINEVEH

Jonah was a prophet in Israel.
He told people the word of God.
One day, God called to him:
"Jonah, Jonah.
Go to Nineveh.
Go to Nineveh right away.

"The people of Nineveh are wicked.
They worship idols.
They are unkind to each other.
Go to Nineveh.
Say to them:
'Hear the word of God
and change your ways.
Change your ways, or God will punish you.
You are not living by My commandments.'"

Jonah did not answer God.
"I do not want to go to Nineveh.
I do not want to prophesy.
People will not like to hear me say:
'You are doing wrong, change your ways.'
I will turn my back to Nineveh.
I will run away from God,
and I will go to Tarshish," said Jonah.
"I will not have to be a prophet there."

Jonah got on a ship that was going to Tarshish.
He found a bed.
He went to sleep.
The ship set sail for Tarshish.
But suddenly the wind blew.

It blew the waves so hard
that people fell out of their beds.

But did Jonah wake up?
No, he went right on sleeping.
The wind blew the waves so hard
that the ship almost tipped over.
But did Jonah wake up?
No. He went right on sleeping.
The thunder thundered.
The lightning almost touched the ship.
All the people prayed to their gods.
"Help us, help us," they prayed.
But not Jonah.
Jonah was still asleep.
All the sailors prayed to their gods.
"Help us, help us," they prayed.
But the sea was still angry.
The wind still blew.
And the people were very
frightened.

"Look through the boat," said the captain.
"Maybe someone is still in bed."
"Impossible," said the sailors.
"Who could sleep through all this wind?
Who could sleep with the frightening lightning?"
"Look," said the captain.
"Maybe you will find someone.
We will have him pray, too."

The sailors looked.
They looked in all the beds.
"This is foolish," said the sailors.
"How could anyone sleep through such a storm?"
But they kept looking.
In a few minutes, they found Jonah—sound asleep.
"Wake up, wake up," shouted the sailors.
"Wake up and pray to your God.
The waves are as high as houses.
The thunder and lightning are frightening.
Wake up and pray to your God."
Jonah woke up.
He felt the boat rock.
He saw the lightning flash.
"Oh," thought Jonah, "I should never have run away.
God is everywhere.
He is watching me now.
He is punishing me because I did not go to Nineveh.
He is punishing these poor people, too.
What can I do? What can I do?
What can I do?"

Jonah went to the captain.
"Throw me into the sea." said Jonah.

"The sea will not be angry anymore.
The storm will go away.
And you will reach dry land safely."

"No," said the captain.
You will drown.
You cannot swim in such an angry sea.
I will not throw you in."

The sea got angrier and angrier.
The waves poured water over the ship.
The people were frightened.

"Throw me into the sea," said Jonah again.
"The sea will not be angry anymore.
The storm will go away.
And you will reach dry land safely."

"Very well," said the captain,
"but I did not want to do this."
One sailor took Jonah's arms.
One sailor took Jonah's feet.
They threw him into the sea.

The waves got smaller and smaller.
The thunder stopped roaring.
The lightning did not flash anymore.
The rain stopped,
and the sun came out.
The ship got to dry land safely.
But poor Jonah.
He swam
and he swam
and he swam.

He swam until he was too tired to move his arms.
He swam till his feet were too tired
to kick.
But did he swim towards Nineveh?
Not at all.
"I may drown," thought Jonah,
"but I will *not* go to Nineveh."

Jonah floated and floated
till he was cold and sleepy.
"O God," thought Jonah.
"Save me.
Put me back on dry land."

And then Jonah closed his eyes.
He thought something strong lifted him up.
A long time seemed to go by.
When he opened his eyes, he was lying on a beach.
"God has answered my prayer," thought Jonah.
"But how? I wonder how?

Perhaps God sent a giant fish to lift me up
and drop me back on dry land.
Maybe God sent a big wave to throw me on the beach.
It does not matter how I got here.
It only matters that God put me here.
Now I know I cannot run away from God.
Now I will go to Nineveh."

JONAH IS ANGRY

God called Jonah again.
"Go to Nineveh," said God,
"that great and important city.
The people of Nineveh think about themselves.
They do not think about each other.
They think about good times.
They do not think about God."

So Jonah set out for Nineveh.
"What will I say to the people?" thought Jonah.
"Go to Nineveh, that great and important city.
Say to the people:
Hear the word of God,"
said a voice.

"Say to the people:
'Change your ways.
Love your neighbor.
Worship *Adonai*, and Nineveh will be saved.
Change your ways, or God will punish you.' "

"God will destroy Nineveh," Jonah called out.
"God will destroy Nineveh because the people do
wrong.
Change your ways, return to *Adonai*,
or your city will be destroyed."

The beggars heard Jonah's words.
"We have done nothing wrong," they said.
The poor people heard Jonah's words.
"We have done nothing wrong," they said.
The rich people heard Jonah's words, too.
"We have done nothing wrong at all,"
they said.
The king heard Jonah's words.
He made an announcement.
"Jonah is right," said the king.
"We have been wicked.
We must change our ways.
Everyone in Nineveh must pray to *Adonai*.
Everyone in Nineveh must fast.
Adonai will show us what is wrong
and forgive us.
Maybe *Adonai* will not harm our city."

All the people of Nineveh fasted.
All the people of Nineveh prayed to God.
Then the people changed their ways.
The people began to love each other.

And they began to help each other.
"Jonah," called *Adonai*.
"Say to the people of Nineveh:
'Do not be afraid.
You have changed your ways.
Adonai will forgive you.'"

"I knew it!
I knew it!" cried Jonah.
"I knew You'd forgive them.
I knew I would come here for nothing.
Why did I have to come so far?
Why did You make me threaten the people?
You did not want to punish them.
I can never go to Nineveh.
I am too ashamed.
Let me die now.
I cannot be Your prophet.
You forgive too many people."
"Jonah," said the voice of God.
"Are you right to be so angry?"

Jonah did not answer *Adonai*.
Jonah went outside the city and sat down by the gate.
"Maybe now *Adonai* will have a change of mind,"
thought Jonah.
"*Adonai* may still destroy this city."
Jonah sat down under a large gourd plant.
"I will sit here and wait," thought Jonah.
"The gourd will shade me from the sun."
The gourd shaded Jonah all that day.

The next morning, the gourd plant lay on the ground.
It was all dried up.

A worm had sucked out the juice of the gourd.
Jonah sat by the gate in the hot sun.
There was no gourd plant to shade him.
Jonah got hotter and hotter.
"O God," Jonah called out.

"Are you very angry about the gourd?" asked God.

"I am. I am very angry.
The plant gave me shade.
Its leaves kept me cool.
Now it is gone.
The sun is baking me.
It is better for me to die than live.
Why did You dry up the gourd?" asked Jonah.

"The gourd grew up in a day," said God.
"It died in a day.
It was only a plant, but it shaded you
from the sun.
Nineveh is more than a plant.
Nineveh is a great and important city.
Many people built it.
Many people live in it.
They are all My children.
I love them all.
The people of Nineveh did wrong.
But they changed their ways.
And they came back to Me.
Should I destroy them now?
No. I love them, and I will forgive them.
I will give them another chance to be good people."

Jonah stood up.

"I did wrong, too.
I loved myself so much.
I loved a plant more than I loved people.
Forgive me, O *Adonai*."
He stood up.
He walked away from Nineveh.
He went back to the Land of Israel.
But he never was a prophet again.

A psalm of praise.

Shout for *Adonai*, all the earth;
    worship *Adonai* in gladness;
    come into *Adonai*'s presence with singing.
Believe that *Adonai* is God;
    God made us and we are God's,
    God's people, the flock God tends.
Enter God's gates with thanksgiving,
    God's courts with praise.
Praise *Adonai*!
Bless God's name!
For *Adonai* is good;
    God's mercy endures forever;
    God's faithfulness is for all generations.

Psalms 100

ESTHER

Is your name Estelle? or Star? or Myrtle? or Hadassah?
Every girl named Estelle,
every girl named Star,
every girl named Myrtle,
and every girl named Hadassah
should be very proud indeed.
They should be very proud
because they all were named for a famous queen.
They all were named for Esther, the shining star of her
people.

Once upon a time, Ahasuerus was king of Persia.
Ahasuerus was happy except for one thing.
Ahasuerus wanted a queen.

"I'll get you a queen," said Haman.
Haman was Ahasuerus's prime minister.
He took care of many important things for Ahasuerus.
"She must be very beautiful," said Ahasuerus.
"Beautiful," said Haman.
And she must have dark hair."
"Dark hair...," said Haman.
"She must be thin, too," said Ahasuerus.
"I hate fat women."
"Very well, Your Majesty," said Haman.
"I will send messengers all through Shushan.
I will send messengers throughout Persia.
I will send messengers throughout the world.
They will find you a queen."

The messengers brought back many girls.
All the girls had black hair.

All the girls were thin.
All the girls were beautiful.
"Let the girls parade before me,"
commanded Ahasuerus.
The girls paraded before the king.
"There's a nice looking girl," whispered Haman.
"She's too tall," said Ahasuerus.
"There's another one," whispered Haman.
"I don't like her," said Ahasuerus, "she's too small.
But look over there, Haman.
Look over there.
Here she comes.
Here comes the prettiest girl in the world.
What's her name, Haman?
What's her name?"

Haman stopped the parade.
"You, over there," he shouted, "what's your name?"
The girl looked around.
"I say," Haman shouted, "what's your name?"
"My name is Esther," said the girl.
"Esther," said the king to himself,
"what a beautiful name.
Esther," said the king aloud, "come to me.
Come to me, my dear.
You shall be my queen.
The next queen of Persia."

Esther bowed low.
"Thank you, Your Majesty," she said.
"Thank you very much.
Do you mind if I tell Mordecai?"
"Who is Mordecai?" asked the king.
"Mordecai is my cousin," said Esther.

"We live in a small house in Shushan.
He will be living there alone now.
I want to tell him my wonderful news."

"Little Esther," said Mordecai, "you are a very lucky girl.
But who will take care of you in the palace?
And how will you remember to pray to your God?"
"Miriam will take care of me," said Esther.
"She has taken care of me since I was a baby.
The king says she may live in the palace, too.
And, Mordecai, you can visit me.

Visit me every day.
Tell me the news.
And, if I forget, remind me to pray to our God."
So Esther became the queen.
Miriam took good care of her.
Mordecai came to see her every day.
She was very happy.

But, one day, Mordecai had bad news.
"Esther," said Mordecai, "I want you to be happy.
I want you to be safe.
But your people are in danger.
Haman wants to kill us all."
"What can I do about it?" asked Esther.
"You can go to the king," said Mordecai.
"You can go to the king.
Tell him about Haman.
Maybe you can save your people."
"Let someone else go," said Esther.
"I cannot go to the king.
The law says the king must call me first.
Do you want me to die?
The king can kill anyone who comes
if the king does not call first.
That is the law."
"I know the law," said Mordecai.
"But no one else can go.
The king will not listen to anyone else.
Maybe he will listen to you.
Maybe God made you queen of Persia
to save your people now."

Esther did not say anything.

She sat quiet for a long time.
Then she stood up.
"Mordecai," she said, "you are right.
I must go to the king.
I may die.
But, if I die, I die to save my people."

"Miriam," said Esther, "get me my prettiest dress.
And brush my hair till it shines.
I must look my best.
I am going to the king."
"Esther," said Mordecai, "you look beautiful.
The king will listen to you.
Do not be afraid."

So Esther went to see the king.
He was sitting on his throne.
He looked up. He saw Esther.
"Esther, my dear," said Ahasuerus,
"you look prettier than ever.
Did I call for you?"
Esther bowed low before the king.
"No, Your Majesty," she said,
"you did not call for me."
"Why have you come, Esther?" asked the king.
"The law is that I must call you.
But I am not angry."
The king raised his golden sceptre.
"Good," thought Esther.
"The king is not angry.
My life is saved."
"Come, sit beside me on my throne,"
said King Ahasuerus.
"Tell me what you want."

"I have not seen you in a long time," said Esther.
"I miss you.
Will you come to dinner tonight?"
"Is that all you want?" asked the king.
"No," said Esther.
"Please bring Haman with you."
"Haman and I will be delighted to come,"
said the king.
"Thank you," said Esther.
"Good-by until tonight."

That night, the king and Haman came to dinner.
They ate and ate and ate.
They cleaned their plates,
and they asked for more food.
"Mmmmm," said the king
as he finished his meal.
"This is the best dinner I ever ate."
"I'll say," said Haman.
"The very best dinner I ever ate."
"The dinner was so good," said Ahasuerus,
"that I want to thank you for it, Esther.
What would you like?
I will give you anything in the world."

"Save my life," said Esther.
"Your life?
No one would dare to kill you," said the king.
"Someone is planning to kill me and my people.
He has planned to kill us for many days."
"What man would do such a wicked thing?"
asked the king.
"Tell me his name.

I will punish him right away.
Who is he, Esther?
Who is he?"

"You know the man well," said Esther.
"He is sitting in this room right now.
He is sitting next to you right now.
His name is Haman.
This wicked Haman wants to kill all the Jews
in Persia."
"Seize him, guards," said Ahasuerus.
"And be sure that I never see his face again."

"But I will need someone to replace him.
A man that I can trust.
I know.
Your cousin, Mordecai.
He saved my life, and I would like
to reward him.
Mordecai will be our next prime minister."
"Esther," said Mordecai, when he heard the news,
"I must send letters to all the Jews in Persia.
I must tell them how their queen saved their lives."

And that is what Mordecai did.
The Jews in Persia were so happy
that they made that day a holiday.
And it has been a holiday ever since.

THE MYSTERIOUS WRITING

Nebuchadnezzar dreamed dreams.
He dreamed dreams when he was afraid.
"Daniel," said Nebuchadnezzar,
"tell me what my dreams mean."
Daniel told him.
Then Nebuchadnezzar prayed.
He prayed to God.
He changed his ways.
He did not dream so many dreams anymore.

Belshazzar was Nebuchadnezzar's son.
He was king after Nebuchadnezzar.
Did he learn anything from his father?
Oh, no!
He was proud of his fine clothes.
He was proud of his wonderful jewels.
He was very proud of his wonderful parties.
He did not think of his people.
He did not pray to God.
He thought only of himself.
He thought only of giving parties.
Parties, parties, parties—all the time.

One night, Belshazzar gave
a tremendous party.
One thousand people came to eat with Belshazzar.
One thousand people came to drink with Belshazzar.
One thousand people came to dance
at Belshazzar's party.
They had a wonderful time,
singing, dancing, and laughing.

In the middle of the fun, the king shouted, "Quiet.
Quiet all of you.
That writing!" said the king.
The people looked.
"On the wall," said the king.
"That finger writing on the wall."

The people looked again.
Nobody saw a finger.
Nobody saw any writing.
Only a painted wall with nothing at all on it.
"Wise ones," said the king.
"What does this writing mean?"
The wise ones shook their heads.
They did not see any writing.
"We do not know what the writing means,"
they said.
"What kind of wise ones are you?" roared the king.

"Magicians, tell me what this writing means?"
The magicians did not see any writing either.
"We do not know either," said the magicians.
"But call for Daniel.
Daniel will tell you all about it.
Daniel knows everything."

Get Daniel," said Belshazzar.
"I will give him a purple robe.
He may wear a gold chain around his neck.
Tell him to hurry to me and read this writing."
Daniel came to the king.
"See that writing on the wall?
Read it.

Read it to me, and I will dress you in purple.
Read it to me, and I will give you a gold chain."
Daniel looked at the wall.
"My wise ones cannot read it," said Belshazzar.
"My magicians cannot read it.
But you understand everything.
Please read it to me."

"I do not want your gifts," said Daniel.
"But I will read the writing for you.
Mene mene, tekel ufarsin," read Daniel.
"O king, your father, Nebuchadnezzar, was great.
He had power over many people.
Everyone was afraid of him.
He was so proud that he took
 the gold cups from Solomon's Temple.
He was too proud.
He was too cruel.
So God punished him.
He was sorry.
And God did not punish anymore.

"You, Belshazzar, have not learned.
You are too proud.
You are so proud that you drink your wine
from the gold cups of Solomon's Temple.
You are selfish.
You do not think about your people.
You think of parties, but you do not think
of your country.
You think of parties, but you do not think
of God.
God has sent you this message:

'*Mene mene, tekel ufarsin.*'
The days of your kingdom are over.
The Persians will take it away."

"Dress this man in purple," commanded Belshazzar.
"Put a gold chain around his neck.
Make him a ruler of the kingdom."

"God has spoken to you, Belshazzar.
When God spoke to Nebuchadnezzar," said Daniel,
"Nebuchadnezzar changed his ways.
And God forgave him.
What about you, Belshazzar?
What will you do now?"

Belshazzar laughed.
"Let the music play," commanded Belshazzar.
"Let the wine come in.
Let the people make merry."

Belshazzar did not change his ways.
He would not change his ways.
That night, when everyone was asleep,
some Persian soldiers stole into the palace.
They killed Belshazzar.
They overcame his kingdom.
And the king of Persia ruled in his place.

DANIEL IN THE LIONS' DEN

Daniel was a wonderful person.
The Jews loved Daniel.
They told many wonderful stories about him.
When they were sad,
they had Daniel do things no one ever could.
But his deeds gave them courage to worship God
and help each other.
"Daniel in the Lions' Den" is one of these stories.

Maybe it couldn't happen to you,
but it will still give you courage.

"King Darius, live forever!"
said the princes of Babylonia.
"You are the strongest ruler in the world.
You are the best ruler in the world.
Everyone should obey you."

"That is true," said Darius.
"That is very true."
"Everyone should pray to your god,"
said the princes again.
"That is true," said Darius.
"You all know that is true,"
"King Darius, we have sad news for you,"
said one of the princes.
"We did not want to tell you our news,"
said another prince.
"But you really must know what is going on."

"What do you know?" asked Darius.
"What do you know that I should know?

Tell me at once."

"We did not want to tell you,"
said one prince.
"We know you love Daniel very much,"
said another prince.
"What about Daniel?" roared the king.
"He prays to his God three times a day,"
said the princes.
"He cannot pray to his God
and pray to your god, too."

"But Daniel always helps me," said Darius.
"He tells me things I need to know.
He understands things you cannot explain.
He is the best governor in Persia."
"But he prays to his God,"
said the princes.
"Not to yours."

"Still," said Darius, "he always helps me."
"You made a law," said the princes.
"And even the ruler must obey his laws.
You made a law that everyone must pray to your god.
Daniel does not pray to your god at all.
Daniel prays to his God alone.
He prays three times every day to his God.
Ask him.
He will tell you."

King Darius called Daniel.
"Daniel," said the king, "is it true?
Do you pray to your God and not to mine?"
Daniel stood up straight.

Daniel stood up tall.
"Yes," said Daniel, "I do.
I pray only to the Living God."

"Do you know my new law?" said the king.
"No one may worship any god except my god."
"I know the law," said Daniel.
"But my God is the Living God
who guards you and me.
My God helps everyone.

I will always pray to my God."
"Daniel," said the king,
"we have been good friends.
But I cannot change the law.
Even the king must obey it.
Everyone must worship my god.
You do not worship my god
so I must punish you.
I must throw you into a den of lions."
"I understand," said Daniel,
"but you will see, Darius.
God knows I am right
and will take care of me."

The king's guards took Daniel.
They threw him into the lions' den.
"Grrr—Grrr—Grrr," roared the lions.
"Those hungry lions will eat Daniel right away,"
thought the king.
"I will have no Daniel to help me
when I do not know what else to do.
No one else understands
all the things Daniel knows.
I will miss him very much."

The next morning, the king
went to the lions' den again.
"Open the door of the den," commanded the king.
The guards opened the door.
"Daniel," called the king,
"has your God saved you from the lions?"

Daniel stepped out of the den.
"Yes, my king.
Adonai has saved me.
I did nothing wrong.
So *Adonai* saved me from the lions."
"Your God is very wonderful," said the king.
"I will pray to your God.
I will tell my people about your God, too."

Darius issued an order.
It went all over the land.
Daniel helped Darius for many, many years,
and he prayed to God all the days of his life.

JOB

Once upon a time, there lived a man named Job.
Job was a very happy man.
"God has blessed me with a wonderful wife,"
said Job.
"God has blessed me with many children.
God has blessed me with many sheep."
Every day, Job fed the poor.
Every day, he took care of the sick
and helped the stranger.
Every day, Job prayed to God
and God was good to Job.

But, one day, enemies came.
They stole Job's oxen.
All of them.
"Bad luck," said Job.
But he blessed God all the same.
The next day, lightning fell from heaven.
It killed Job's sheep.
It killed his shepherds.
"My sheep, my sheep," cried Job.
"And my poor shepherds.
How will I get more flocks?" asked Job.
"Where will I find shepherds to take care of them?"
But Job blessed God all the same.
The next day, more trouble came to Job.
His children were together.
They were eating.
They were talking, and
they were laughing.
Suddenly a strong wind came up.

It shook the trees.
And the trees fell down.
It moved the house,
and the house fell down, too.
It fell on Job's children.
Job's children all died.
Job was very sad.
But he did not complain.
He blessed God's name all the same.
"Job, Job, what shall we do now?"
cried his wife.

"I can do without oxen.
I can do without sheep.
But I cannot do without my children."
"Let us pray to God," said Job.
He stretched out his hands.
"*Adonai* gives, and
Adonai takes away.
Blessed be the name of God," prayed Job.

The next morning, Job woke up.
"I feel sick," he said.
"My legs hurt.
My arms hurt.
I hurt all over."

Job's wife looked at him.
"Boils," said his wife.
"Boils all over you.
Do they hurt very much?"
"They do," said Job.
"They hurt when I stand.
They hurt when I sit.

They hurt when I lie down."
"Do you still trust in *Adonai*?"
asked his wife.
"Do you still believe in *Adonai*?"

"I believed in *Adonai* when *Adonai* sent me good
things," said Job.
"Now I need *Adonai* even more."

Job had three good friends.
"Poor Job," said the first friend.
"Job is very sick," said the second friend.
"Let us visit Job," said the third friend.
"Maybe we can cheer him up."

The friends sat down with Job.
They sat down all that day.
They sat down all the next.
They did not move.
They did not say a word.
For seven days, they all sat quietly.
No one said a word.

On the seventh day, Job spoke.
"Why was I born?" asked Job.
"Why do I have troubles?"
"*Adonai* helps good people, Job,"
said the first friend.
"You tell us that all the time.
Trust in *Adonai*.
Do good, Job,
and *Adonai* will make you well.
Remember, *Adonai* helps all good people."
"I am good," said Job.

"I cannot understand why *Adonai* sends trouble to me."

The second friend said,
"Job, Job, what are you saying?
Are you saying that God is unfair?
We live good lives.
God does not send us troubles.
We do wrong.
God punishes us.
Think, Job, think.
You must have done something wrong.
Change your ways.
And God will help you once again."

"Why should I change my ways?" asked Job.
"I do nothing wrong.
I feed the poor.
I take care of the sick.
I help the stranger.
God knows I am good.
Why does God send me trouble?
I do not understand God."

"You do good, Job.
You do good all the time," said a third friend.
"But do you think good?
Do you think good in your heart?
Do you pray to God every day?
Ask God to help you.
God will take away your troubles.
You will not have them anymore."

"I do what is right," said Job.

"I think what is right.
I pray to God every day.
Why does God send trouble to me?
I do not understand God.
Some wicked people live in beautiful houses.
They eat fine food.
They have children and grandchildren
to make them happy.
They do not have any troubles.
You, my three good friends,
you do not have any troubles either.
Are you any better than I?"

Everything was quiet again.
The three friends did not know what to say.
They did not know how to answer Job.
They did not know how to make him feel better.

All of a sudden, a black cloud
made the sky dark.
The cloud whirled around, and around, and around.
"A whirlwind," cried the friends.
They fell flat on their faces.
Did Job fall flat on his face?
No. He did not.
He stood up.

Job felt the wind whirl stronger and stronger.
He watched the cloud move faster and faster.
But still Job stood up.
Job looked at the wind.
He looked straight into the middle
of the whirling wind.

And, as he looked,
he heard God speak to him.
And this is what God said to Job:
"What man asks questions of *Adonai*?
What man asks questions
but cannot understand the answers?
Stand before Me, Job.
Stand up straight....
Answer some questions for Me.
Did you make the sun and stars?"
"No," said Job in a whisper.
"Did you make the oceans or the dry land?"
"No," said Job in a small voice.
"Did you make the flowers and the animals?"
asked the voice of God.
"No, no, no," said Job.
"I did not make any of these things."
"Did you make a human being
who thinks, who loves, who understands?
Did you ever make a human being, Job?"
"No," said Job, "I did not make a human being."

Job bowed his head.
He did not say a word.
Everything was quiet.
Job raised his head again.

He raised his hands to the sky.
"O *Adonai*," said Job.
"You are greater than I.
You are wiser than I.
You understand things too wonderful for me.
I spoke once," said Job.
"I spoke twice.
But I will not speak again.
I will not question things too wonderful for me.
I thought I could know all about You.
I thought I could understand all about You.
I was too proud.
I did not know how little I really knew.
I do not have to know
everything about You.
I will not always understand
all the things You do.
But I will trust You always,
for You understand things
that are too wonderful for me."

The whirlwind grew still.
The wind died down.
The sky grew light again.
Job sat down.
He began to pray.
"*Adonai* gives, and *Adonai* takes away.
Blessed be the name of God," prayed Job.

Job felt better.
He got well again.
He worked hard.
He trusted in *Adonai*.

He grew rich again.
He had many flocks.
He had many children.
He lived with his children,
his grandchildren, and his great-grandchildren.
He lived happily ever after.

...Give me neither poverty nor riches....

Proverbs 30:8

AT THE TOP OF THE MOUNTAIN

Two men were resting.
They were sitting under a big tree.
They were looking at their gardens.
"Your garden is beautiful, Jacob.
Your plants always grow straight and tall,"
said the first man.
"Your string beans are large and green.
Your cucumbers are juicy and sweet.
I work in my garden, too.
I work hard in my garden.
I pull out the weeds.
New weeds grow up.
I straighten my plants.
They fall over once more.
I am just unlucky."

"No, David, you are not unlucky,"
said Jacob.
"Gardening is hard work.
I do not pull weeds once.
I pull them every day.
I tie up my plants if they get too tall.
I pick off the dead leaves.
I give them lots of water.
I work with them every day.
Come, I will help you tie up your plants.
I will show you the weeds.
You will have a beautiful garden, too."

"Thank you," said David.
The two men started to work in the garden.

Other people came by.
They saw the men working in the garden.
They all stopped to watch.
More and more people stopped.
Soon a crowd of people was watching them.
"How wonderful!" they said.
"One helps the other with the garden."

"Now," said Jacob,
"we have tied up all the plants.
We have taken out
all the weeds for today.
Let us look at your garden now."
The two men stood up.
"It is beautiful," said David.
"Thank you, my friend."

"Your garden is really beautiful now,"
said a voice in the crowd.
"In this garden, you see the word of God."
The people looked around.
They did not see the word of God.
The gardeners looked up.
They did not see the word of God either.
"It is the prophet," said the crowd.
The people looked.
"You do not see the word of God,"
said the prophet, "but I will show it to you.
Two people helped each other
make this beautiful garden.
They believed in each other,
and they believed their God would help them.
And God did help them.

God blessed their work.
Yesterday, this garden was a garden of weeds.
Today, it is a garden of flowers.

"Listen to the word of God.
You will see it is here in this garden.
'When all believe in Me.
When all remember My commandments.
All people will be brothers and sisters.
They will help each other.
They will love each other.
And they will love their God.
They will not need swords.
They will not need spears.
All will help their fellow human beings.
And no one will be afraid.

" 'People will plant gardens.
They will water and weed and hoe.
They will sit near cool grapevines.
They will sit under shady fig trees.
Everyone will be happy.
No one will be afraid.'
My people, we can make these words come true.
Today they are a dream.
But David and Jacob showed us how to make that
dream come true.

"We must work together for what is good.
We must love each other,
and we must love our God.

"It will take many years for this dream to come true.
Many babies will be born.

Many old people will die.
They will not see the dream come true.
But we can wait, and we can work.
The dream will make us work.
When we are happy, it will make us strong.
When we are sad, it will give us courage.
And we will make it come true."

"I believe it," said David.
"I believe it," said Jacob.
"We believe it," said the people.
"It is our dream now.
We promise God we will never forget it.
And we will never stop trying to make it come true."

Who may ascend the mountain of God?
Why may stand in God's holy place?—
Someone who has clean hands and a pure heart...
   shall receive a blessing from God,
   and justice from God, the Deliverer.

Psalms 24:3-5